IMPROV FOR BUSINESS SUCCESS

How to Build Stronger Teams, Better Leaders, and Winning Strategies Through the Power of Play

Walt Frasier

©2024 Improv Theater LLC All rights reserved.

Contents

Chapter 1: Unleashing the Power of Play: Why Improv Comedy Transforms Businesses 3

Chapter 2: Improv for Team Building: Unleashing the Power of Playful Collaboration 7

    Warm-Up Exercises: 7

    Team-Building Games: 8

    Case Studies: Improv in Action 9

    Measuring the Impact 10

Chapter 3: Improv for Leadership: Embracing Spontaneity, Building Trust, and Inspiring Teams 12

    The Improv Leader: Embodying Key Principles .. 12

    Leadership Exercises: 13

    Applying Improv Principles in Real-World Leadership: 15

Chapter 4: Improv for Sales and Customer Service: Building Rapport, Handling Objections, and Delivering Exceptional Experiences 17

    The Art of Connection: Improv's Secret Weapon 17

    Practical Improv Exercises for Sales and Service Scenarios: 18

    Real-World Examples of Improv in Action: 19

    Measuring the Impact of Improv on Sales and Service: 20

Chapter 5: Implementing Improv in Your Organization: From Workshops to Everyday Interactions 22

    Designing Effective Improv Workshops: 22

Integrating Improv into Everyday Work: 24

Additional Tips: 25

Chapter 6: Conclusion: Embracing the Improv Mindset for Lasting Success 27

Chapter 1: Unleashing the Power of Play: Why Improv Comedy Transforms Businesses

In the fast-paced, high-pressure world of business, it might seem counterintuitive to advocate for play. But the truth is, play is not just for children. It's a fundamental human need that, when embraced, can unlock extraordinary potential within individuals and teams. And one of the most powerful forms of play for the corporate world? Improv comedy.

Why Improv? It's More Than Just Laughs

While improv comedy is undeniably fun and entertaining, its benefits extend far beyond mere amusement. At its core, improv is about:

- **Spontaneity and Adaptability:** The ability to think on your feet and embrace the unexpected is crucial in today's ever-changing business landscape. Improv hones this skill by forcing you to react in the moment, creating solutions and opportunities out of thin air.

- **Active Listening and Collaboration:** Improv is a team sport. It thrives on active listening, building on each other's ideas, and co-creating stories together. These skills are essential for effective communication, teamwork, and innovation within any organization.

- **Saying "Yes, And...":** This foundational improv principle encourages acceptance and building upon ideas, rather than shutting them down. This mindset fosters a positive, collaborative environment where creativity and risk-taking flourish.

- **Building Confidence and Overcoming Fear:** Improv pushes individuals out of their comfort zones, helping them conquer the fear of failure and embrace vulnerability. This newfound confidence translates into stronger communication skills, bolder decision-making, and a willingness to take calculated risks.

The Business Case for Improv

The benefits of improv comedy for businesses are undeniable. Companies that incorporate improv into their training programs and company culture have reported:

- **Increased Creativity and Innovation:** Improv sparks new ideas, encourages outside-the-box thinking, and helps teams find creative solutions to complex problems.

- **Improved Communication and Collaboration:** Teams that play together, work better together. Improv strengthens communication skills, fosters trust, and enhances team cohesion.

- **Enhanced Leadership Skills:** Improv empowers leaders to be more adaptable, decisive, and inspiring by teaching them to embrace uncertainty, think on their feet, and empower their teams.

- **Boosted Sales and Customer Service:** Improv techniques like active listening, building rapport, and handling objections can significantly improve sales performance and customer satisfaction.

- **Greater Employee Engagement and Morale:** Improv is fun! By incorporating play into the workplace, you create a more positive and enjoyable environment, leading to increased employee engagement and reduced turnover.

In the following chapters, we'll delve deeper into the specific benefits of improv for team building, leadership development, sales, and customer service. We'll explore practical exercises and real-world examples to show you how to harness the power of play to transform your organization.

Are you ready to say "Yes, And..." to a more innovative, collaborative, and successful workplace? Then let's dive in!

Chapter 2: Improv for Team Building: Unleashing the Power of Playful Collaboration

Improv comedy is not just about being funny; it's a powerful tool for building strong, collaborative teams. The exercises and games in this chapter are designed to foster trust, enhance communication, and unlock the creative potential within your team.

Warm-Up Exercises:

1. **Zip Zap Zup:** A fast-paced energy-building game where participants pass the words "Zip," "Zap," and "Zup" around a circle, adding physical gestures for each word. This exercise promotes focus, listening, and quick thinking.
2. **Name Game:** Each person states their name followed by an adjective that describes them, starting with the same letter as their name (e.g., "Joyful Jessica," "Daring David"). This

helps team members learn each other's names while adding a personal touch.

3. **One-Word Story:** The team creates a story one word at a time, with each person contributing the next word. This fosters collaboration, active listening, and builds a sense of shared creation.

Team-Building Games:

1. **Group Counting:** The group tries to count to 20 in unison, with each person saying a random number. If two people speak at once, the count starts over. This seemingly simple exercise requires deep listening, collaboration, and non-verbal communication to succeed.

2. **Yes, And... Scene:** Two people start a scene with a simple premise, and each person builds on the other's ideas using the "Yes, And..." principle. This exercise reinforces the power of agreement, collaboration, and building on each other's strengths.

3. **Human Knot:** The team stands in a circle, reaches across and grabs two different people's hands. Then, without letting go, they work together to untangle themselves into a circle. This exercise requires problem-solving, communication, and physical cooperation.

Case Studies: Improv in Action

- **Google:** Google has incorporated improv into its employee training programs to foster creativity, innovation, and collaboration. They've seen improvements in team communication, problem-solving skills, and overall company culture.

- **Pixar:** The renowned animation studio uses improv exercises to spark creativity and generate new ideas for their films. They believe that playfulness and collaboration are essential ingredients for innovation.

- **Southwest Airlines:** Southwest is known for its fun-loving company culture, and improv plays a role in that. They encourage employees to have fun at work, which has led to increased employee satisfaction and customer loyalty.

Measuring the Impact

To assess the effectiveness of improv for team building, consider tracking the following:

- **Communication:** Do team members communicate more openly and effectively?
- **Collaboration:** Are teams working more collaboratively and effectively?
- **Creativity:** Are team members generating more creative ideas and solutions?
- **Trust:** Do team members trust and support each other more?
- **Overall Morale:** Has team morale improved?

By incorporating improv games and exercises into your team-building efforts, you can unlock the power of play to create a more collaborative, innovative, and enjoyable workplace. Remember, the goal is not to create professional comedians, but rather to foster a team culture where everyone feels empowered to contribute, collaborate, and have fun.

Chapter 3: Improv for Leadership: Embracing Spontaneity, Building Trust, and Inspiring Teams

Effective leadership is not about having all the answers or following a script. It's about navigating uncertainty, building trust, and inspiring others to achieve shared goals. These are skills that can be honed and refined through the practice of improv comedy.

The Improv Leader: Embodying Key Principles

- **Adaptability:** Like skilled improvisers, effective leaders embrace change and adapt quickly to new situations. They remain flexible, open-minded, and willing to pivot when necessary.

- **Active Listening:** Great leaders listen deeply to their team members, valuing their input and perspectives. They create a safe space for open communication and collaboration.

- **Collaboration:** Improv is a team effort, and so is leadership. Effective leaders foster a collaborative environment where everyone feels empowered to contribute and take ownership.

- **Saying "Yes, And...":** Leaders who embrace this principle build on their team's ideas, creating a positive and inclusive atmosphere where innovation thrives.

- **Building Trust:** Through vulnerability, authenticity, and a willingness to take risks, improv leaders cultivate trust and psychological safety within their teams.

- **Inspiring Others:** Like compelling improvisers, great leaders inspire their teams with their passion, vision, and ability to motivate others.

Leadership Exercises:

1. **Expert Panel:** A group of participants are assigned to be "experts" on a random topic. They must answer questions from the audience (the rest of the team) spontaneously

and confidently, even if they know nothing about the subject. This exercise builds quick thinking, adaptability, and the ability to speak with authority.

2. **World's Worst...:** Participants take turns offering suggestions for the "World's Worst" of something (e.g., "World's Worst Boss," "World's Worst Sales Pitch"). This exercise encourages creative problem-solving and the ability to find humor in challenging situations.

3. **What Are You Doing?:** Two people begin a scene with one person performing a physical activity. The other person asks, "What are you doing?" The first person must make up a new activity on the spot, and the scene continues with the second person guessing and adapting to the new action. This exercise builds flexibility, adaptability, and the ability to respond to changing circumstances.

4. **Freeze and Justify:** A scene is in progress, and at any point, someone yells "Freeze!" The actors freeze in place, and a new person enters the scene, tapping one of the frozen

actors out. The new actor must justify the frozen position and start a new scene from that point. This exercise builds creativity, storytelling skills, and the ability to take ownership of a situation and move it forward.

Applying Improv Principles in Real-World Leadership:

- **Leading Meetings:** Encourage team members to build on each other's ideas using "Yes, And...". Use improv games as icebreakers or to spark creativity during brainstorming sessions.

- **Giving Feedback:** Practice active listening and acknowledge team members' contributions before offering constructive criticism.

- **Handling Conflict:** Use improv techniques like active listening and finding common ground to de-escalate conflict and reach mutually beneficial solutions.

- **Public Speaking:** Embrace the unexpected during presentations and Q&A sessions. Use humor and storytelling to engage your audience.

By incorporating improv into your leadership development, you can cultivate the adaptability, creativity, and collaboration skills necessary to thrive in today's complex and ever-changing business landscape.

Remember: The most effective leaders are those who empower their teams to be their best. By fostering a playful, collaborative, and supportive environment, you can unlock the full potential of your team and achieve extraordinary results.

Chapter 4: Improv for Sales and Customer Service: Building Rapport, Handling Objections, and Delivering Exceptional Experiences

In the world of sales and customer service, success hinges on building strong relationships and providing exceptional experiences. Improv comedy offers a surprising but powerful set of tools to achieve these goals. By embracing the principles of listening, collaboration, and adaptability, you can transform your interactions with clients and customers.

The Art of Connection: Improv's Secret Weapon

1. **Active Listening:** In improv, active listening is not just about hearing the words; it's about understanding the underlying emotions, needs, and desires. By actively listening to your clients, you gain valuable insights that can help you tailor your solutions and build rapport.

2. **Building Rapport:** Improv teaches you to connect with people on a human level. By using humor, empathy, and genuine curiosity, you can break down barriers and create a sense of trust and connection.

3. **Adaptability:** Sales and customer service interactions are rarely predictable. Improv trains you to think on your feet, adapt to unexpected challenges, and find creative solutions in the moment.

Practical Improv Exercises for Sales and Service Scenarios:

1. **Yes, And... to Objections:** Instead of shutting down objections, use the "Yes, And..." principle to acknowledge the customer's concerns and then build upon them. For example, if a customer says, "Your product is too expensive," you could respond, "Yes, and we offer flexible payment options to make it more affordable."

2. **Active Listening Challenge:** Pair up with a colleague and practice active listening in a

simulated customer interaction. One person plays the customer, while the other practices mirroring their emotions, paraphrasing their statements, and asking clarifying questions.

3. **Improv Role-Play:** Create scenarios based on common customer interactions (e.g., handling complaints, upselling products, resolving conflicts). Practice improvising responses to these scenarios, focusing on active listening, empathy, and problem-solving.

4. **Customer Service Charades:** Write down common customer service phrases or scenarios on index cards. Have team members act out the phrases or scenarios without speaking, while others guess what they are trying to convey. This exercise promotes non-verbal communication skills and empathy.

Real-World Examples of Improv in Action:

- **Zappos:** The online retailer is famous for its exceptional customer service, and improv plays a role in their training. They encourage employees to be themselves, have fun, and build genuine connections with customers.

- **Salesforce:** Salesforce uses improv techniques to help its sales team build rapport with clients, handle objections, and close deals. They believe that improv skills are essential for success in today's competitive market.

- **The Ritz-Carlton:** The luxury hotel chain incorporates improv into its employee training to enhance customer service skills and create memorable guest experiences. They believe that improvisation empowers employees to deliver personalized and genuine service.

Measuring the Impact of Improv on Sales and Service:

- **Customer Satisfaction:** Do customers report higher levels of satisfaction with your interactions?

- **Sales Performance:** Has your sales team seen an increase in closed deals or average deal size?

- **Employee Engagement:** Are your sales and service team members more engaged and enthusiastic about their work?

By embracing improv in your sales and customer service training, you can empower your team to connect with customers on a deeper level, handle challenges with grace, and deliver exceptional experiences that drive loyalty and growth.

Chapter 5: Implementing Improv in Your Organization: From Workshops to Everyday Interactions

Bringing the power of improv into your workplace requires more than just reading about it – it's about taking action. This chapter provides guidance on designing effective improv workshops and incorporating improv principles into your daily routines.

Designing Effective Improv Workshops:

1. **Set Clear Objectives:** What specific skills or outcomes do you want your team to achieve through the workshop? Whether it's improving communication, fostering creativity, or building trust, clearly defined goals will shape the workshop's content and activities.

2. **Tailor to Your Audience:** Consider the size, experience level, and specific needs of your

team. Adapt exercises and games to suit their comfort levels and learning styles.

3. **Start with the Basics:** Begin with foundational improv principles like "Yes, And...", active listening, and collaboration. Introduce warm-up exercises to build trust and create a safe space for experimentation.

4. **Gradually Increase Challenge:** As the workshop progresses, introduce more complex exercises that focus on specific skills like storytelling, problem-solving, and adaptability.

5. **Facilitate, Don't Lead:** The facilitator's role is to guide, encourage, and create a safe and supportive environment. Avoid lecturing or dictating; instead, foster a collaborative atmosphere where participants can learn from each other.

6. **Debrief and Reflect:** After each exercise, take time to debrief and discuss the experience. What worked well? What could be improved? How can the learnings be applied to real-world scenarios?

7. **Provide Take-Home Tools:** Offer participants resources like handouts, worksheets, or a list of improv games they can practice on their own.

Integrating Improv into Everyday Work:

1. **"Yes, And..." Meetings:** Encourage team members to build on each other's ideas during meetings. Start with a "Yes, And..." round where everyone shares a positive observation about a project or idea.

2. **Improv Icebreakers:** Use improv games like "One-Word Story" or "Zip Zap Zup" to break the ice and energize the team before meetings or workshops.

3. **Improv Presentations:** Encourage presenters to practice improvisational storytelling to make their presentations more engaging and relatable.

4. **Improv Brainstorming:** Use improv exercises like "World's Worst..." or "Expert Panel" to

spark creativity and generate new ideas during brainstorming sessions.

5. **Improv Customer Service:** Encourage customer service representatives to practice active listening and empathetic communication. Use improv role-play to simulate challenging customer interactions.

Additional Tips:

- **Start Small:** Begin with short improv sessions or exercises to build comfort and confidence.

- **Lead by Example:** Managers and leaders should actively participate in improv activities to demonstrate their commitment and create a culture of play.

- **Make it Fun:** Improv should be enjoyable! Choose games and exercises that are engaging and relevant to your team's interests.

- **Celebrate Success:** Acknowledge and reward teams and individuals who demonstrate improv principles in their work.

By implementing these strategies, you can create a workplace culture where improv becomes a natural part of your team's communication and collaboration. Remember, the goal is not to turn your employees into professional comedians, but to empower them with the skills and mindset to be more adaptable, creative, and collaborative in all aspects of their work.

Chapter 6: Conclusion: Embracing the Improv Mindset for Lasting Success

Throughout this ebook, we've explored the transformative power of improv comedy for team building, leadership development, sales, and customer service. We've seen how the core principles of "Yes, And...", active listening, collaboration, and adaptability can unlock the full potential of individuals and teams.

Key Takeaways:

- **Improv is Play with a Purpose:** While it's undeniably fun, improv is a serious tool for developing essential skills like communication, creativity, problem-solving, and adaptability.

- **Improv Builds Stronger Teams:** Through playful exercises and games, improv fosters trust, collaboration, and a shared sense of purpose within teams.

- **Improv Creates Better Leaders:** The improvisational mindset empowers leaders to embrace change, listen deeply, and inspire their teams to achieve extraordinary results.

- **Improv Transforms Sales and Service:** By building rapport, handling objections with grace, and adapting to unexpected challenges, improv elevates the customer experience.

- **Improv is a Journey, Not a Destination:** The skills and mindset cultivated through improv are not a one-time fix. They require ongoing practice and integration into your daily work.

Your Call to Action:

If you're ready to unleash the power of play in your organization, here are a few steps you can take:

1. **Book a Workshop:** Experience the transformative power of improv firsthand by booking a workshop for your team. Our experienced facilitators will guide you through a fun and engaging experience that will leave your team feeling energized, connected, and equipped with new skills.

2. **Incorporate Improv into Your Daily Routine:** Start small by incorporating improv games and exercises into your meetings, presentations, and team interactions. Encourage a culture of playfulness and experimentation.

3. **Explore Further Resources:** Dive deeper into the world of improv by reading books, watching videos, and attending performances. (You can find a wealth of resources on the website of the New York Improv Theater!)

4. **Become a Lifelong Learner:** Improv is a continuous journey of growth and discovery. Embrace the improv mindset and never stop learning, adapting, and playing.

The Future is Yours to Improvise:

The skills you develop through improv are not just for the stage; they are essential tools for navigating the complexities of the modern workplace. By embracing the improv mindset, you can build stronger teams, become a more effective leader, and create a more positive and productive work environment.

So, what are you waiting for? Say "Yes, And..." to the power of improv and unlock your team's full potential!

Addendum A: The New York Improv Theater's Typical Improv Workshop

No substitute exists for the experiential learning that comes from playing improv games. Engaging in these activities firsthand fosters the skills that countless books and lectures merely discuss.

At the New York Improv Theater, we host corporate groups weekly in Times Square and travel to events from D.C. to Boston and beyond. We employ a version of the workshop outlined in this eBook to teach team building, leadership, sales, and service skills. While we customize our workshops to your team's specific needs and challenges, the specific games we play are less important than the principles they embody. There are thousands of improv games to choose from, and we often adjust our selection based on your team's skill levels and evolving needs.

Our Three #1s:

We begin every session by emphasizing three foundational principles:

1. **Walter's #1 Rule: HAVE FUN but never at another's expense.** Improv thrives on a playful and supportive atmosphere where everyone feels safe to take risks and be themselves.

2. **#1 Improv Rule: "YES! AND…"** ALWAYS SAY "YES!" And… follow up with words and actions in support of your team, their ideas and actions. This principle teaches **psychological safety**, the number one factor in team success. By focusing on making your teammates look good, you create a collaborative environment where everyone feels empowered to contribute.

3. **#1 Comedy Skill: Listening!** Listening with your eyes. Listening with the willingness to change. This is also the number one skill in a great leader. Active listening involves not just hearing the words, but also understanding the underlying emotions and intentions. It's about listening with your eyes and being open to changing your perspective based on what you hear.

Warm-Up Games:

1. **Zip Zap Zup:** The classic game warms us up individually and as a team, teaching us to listen and respond quickly as we pass around simple words and gestures.

2. **Pass the Face:** An improv version of telephone, where players pass around a silly face, gesture, and sound. This exercise highlights the importance of non-verbal communication and observation.

3. **What Are You Doing?:** We break out of our shells a bit with silly pantomimes – swimming, biking, running, rock climbing – to spark creativity and spontaneity.

Team-Building Games:

4. **Ten Scenes Ten Minutes:** In smaller teams scattered around the room, players spontaneously create a series of simple conversations based on a location or scenario. This activity builds quick thinking, collaboration, and storytelling skills.

5. **Eight Things or Categories of Eight:** Each player is given a topic to list eight things, while the team encouragingly counts to eight after each offer. This game promotes creative thinking, quick recall, and supportive teamwork.

6. **One Word Story:** Players create a short story, one word at a time. This exercise fosters collaboration, active listening, and builds a sense of shared creation.

7. **Yes! And... Short Stories:** Players create mini-stories one sentence at a time, starting with the words "Yes! And..." This exercise reinforces the power of agreement, collaboration, and building on each other's ideas.

8. **I Am a Tree:** We learn to make simple choices, listen, and "Yes, And..." as we build a series of pictures. This game develops trust, non-verbal communication, and the ability to create a shared vision.

Masterclass of Performance Games:

Unlike most corporate training improv companies, we believe in ending the session with a taste of actual performance games you might see in a show like "Whose Line Is It Anyway?" or performed by local troupes, including our own off-Broadway show. These games showcase the potential of improv and demonstrate how far the team has come during the session. Many fear improv as the ultimate expression of the unknown, but we show that creating stories without a net is easier than we think. We simply have some fun for the final 30 minutes of a 2-hour workshop as smaller groups take the stage to create original skits and songs – just like we do in our professional shows!

The New York Improv Theater Experience:

By experiencing the power of improv firsthand, you'll gain a deeper understanding of how these principles can transform your team's communication, collaboration, and overall performance. Our workshops are designed to be fun, engaging, and tailored to your specific needs. We'll work with you to create a customized experience that will leave your team feeling energized, connected, and equipped with the skills they need to succeed.

Ready to take the next step?

Contact the New York Improv Theater today to learn more about our corporate workshops and how we can help your team unleash its full potential!

Improv Theater LLC
www.newyorkimprovtheater.com
212.568.6560
eightimprov@gmail.com

Addendum B: About the Author and Improv Theater LLC

Walt Frasier:

Walt Frasier is a veteran performer with over 25 years of professional experience in comedy, theater, and music. His impressive resume includes appearances on MTV's "Stankervision," "Late Nite with David Letterman," TruTV's "Friends of the People," and HBO's "Pause with Sam Jay." He has also acted in numerous television shows and commercials, including NBC's "Blacklist," CBS's "Blue Bloods," USA's "Royal Pains," Netflix's "Lilyhammer," and Nickelodeon's "Naked Brothers Band." With thousands of live performances worldwide under his belt, Walt Frasier brings a wealth of experience and expertise to the world of improv comedy.

The New York Improv Theater:

The New York Improv Theater is your one-stop edutainment center for corporate team building, office/holiday parties, and more. Our comedy shows and workshops deliver high-impact results, helping teams unlock their full potential through the power of play. Our diverse client roster includes Google, Effy, Merck, Mercedes Benz, META /Facebook, TikTok / Bytedance, JP Morgan Chase, Accenture, Morgan Stanley, Twitter, Roblox, Rimowa, El Digital, Accenture, Datadog HQ, Milbank, BING/Microsoft, Band of America – Merrill Lynch, Home Depot, Ernst & Young, Johnson & Johnson, Louis Vuitton, Coach, UBS, BDO, AMEX, Master Card, Macy's, 360i, IBM, GM, Kraft, UNILEAVER, HBO, Prudential, Convene, Conference Board and many more… (NYC DOE VENDORS)

EIGHT IS NEVER ENOUGH:

Our flagship show, EIGHT IS NEVER ENOUGH, has been delighting audiences with interactive musical comedy improv since 2002. The show is based entirely on audience suggestions and participation, making each performance unique and unforgettable. We perform live from Times Square and tour nationwide, bringing the joy of improv to clubs, theaters, corporate events, colleges, schools, and private functions.

Books by Walt Frasier:

Comedy 4 Life Series
- *Stand Up Comedy*
- *Sketch Comedy*
- *Quit Your Day Job*

Improv 4 Kids Series: Creative writing for kids and teens
- *Stand Up Comedy*
- *Improv on Zoom*

www.ingramcontent.com/pod-product-compliance
Lightning Source LLC
Chambersburg PA
CBHW070954220526
45471CB00007B/3029